Please return/renew this item by the last date shown
Thank you for using your library

Wolverhampton Libraries ♻

YORK PRESS
322 Old Brompton Road, London SW5 9JH

ADDISON WESLEY LONGMAN LIMITED
Edinburgh Gate, Harlow,
Essex CM20 2JE, United Kingdom
Associated companies, branches and representatives throughout the world

First published 1997

ISBN 0–582–31402–X

Designed by Vicki Pacey, Trojan Horse
Illustrated by Adam Stower
Map by Val Hill
Phototypeset by Gem Graphics, Trenance, Mawgan Porth, Cornwall
Produced by Longman Asia Limited, Hong Kong

CONTENTS

PREFACE

York Notes are designed to give you a broader perspective on works of literature studied at GCSE and equivalent levels. We have carried out extensive research into the needs of the modern literature student prior to publishing this new edition. Our research showed that no existing series fully met students' requirements. Rather than present a single authoritative approach, we have provided alternative viewpoints, empowering students to reach their own interpretations of the text. York Notes provide a close examination of the work and include biographical and historical background, summaries, glossaries, analyses of characters, themes, structure and language, cultural connections and literary terms.

If you look at the Contents page you will see the structure for the series. However, there's no need to read from the beginning to the end as you would with a novel, play, poem or short story. Use the Notes in the way that suits you. Our aim is to help you with your understanding of the work, not to dictate how you should learn.

York Notes are written by English teachers and examiners, with an expert knowledge of the subject. They show you how to succeed in coursework and examination assignments, guiding you through the text and offering practical advice. Questions and comments will extend, test and reinforce your knowledge. Attractive colour design and illustrations improve clarity and understanding, making these Notes easy to use and handy for quick reference.

York Notes are ideal for:
- Essay writing
- Exam preparation
- Class discussion

The author of these Notes is Chrissie Wright, an ex head of English and deputy head teacher of a school in Stockton. She was educated at Durham University and the Open University, and works as a senior examiner for GCSE English and Literature.

The text used in these Notes is published by Penguin Books, 1968.

Health Warning: **This study guide will enhance your understanding, but should not replace the reading of the original text and/or study in class.**

PART ONE

INTRODUCTION

HOW TO STUDY A NOVEL

You have bought this book because you wanted to study a novel on your own. This may supplement classwork.

- You will need to read the novel several times. Start by reading it quickly for pleasure, then read it slowly and carefully. Further readings will generate new ideas and help you to memorise the details of the story.
- Make careful notes on themes, plot and characters of the novel. The plot will change some of the characters. Who changes?
- The novel may not present events chronologically. Does the novel you are reading begin at the beginning of the story or does it contain flashbacks and a muddled time sequence? Can you think why?
- How is the story told? Is it narrated by one of the characters or by an all-seeing ('omniscient') narrator?
- Does the same person tell the story all the way through? Or do we see the events through the minds and feelings of a number of different people.
- Which characters does the narrator like? Which characters do you like or dislike? Do your sympathies change during the course of the book? Why? When?
- Any piece of writing (including your notes and essays) is the result of thousands of choices. No book had to be written in just one way: the author could have chosen other words, other phrases, other characters, other events. How could the author of your novel have written the story differently? If events were recounted by a minor character how would this change the novel?

Studying on your own requires self-discipline and a carefully thought-out work plan in order to be effective. Good luck.

Barry Hines was born in the mining village of Hoyland Common, near Barnsley in Yorkshire. He was educated at Ecclesfield grammar school, where he was selected to play for the England Grammar Schools' football team. After leaving school he worked as an apprentice mining surveyor and played football for Barnsley, mainly in the 'A' team. He studied physical education at Loughborough Training College, before embarking on a career as a teacher which lasted several years, working in London and his native South Yorkshire. He left teaching to become a full time novelist and playwright.

His first novel, *The Blinder*, was published in 1966 and is set in the world of football. *A Kestrel for a Knave* followed in 1968 and was an immediate bestseller. In 1970 it was made into a popular film – *Kes* – by director Ken Loach.

Other novels by Barry Hines include *First Signs* (1972), *The Gamekeeper* (1975), *The Price of Coal* (1979) and *Looks and Smiles* which was filmed in 1981, when it won the Prize for Contemporary Cinema at the Cannes Film Festival. Perhaps Hines's most famous play for television was the documentary-style *Threads* (1983) based on the theme of global nuclear war and set in Sheffield, for which he won a BAFTA award. Since then he has completed two further novels *Unfinished Business* and *The Heart of It*.

Barry Hines lives and works in Sheffield, and is a Fellow of Sheffield Hallam University.

CONTEXT & SETTING

As an early novel in Barry Hines's career, *A Kestrel for a Knave* contains material which is closely related to his early background in South Yorkshire.

SETTING

It is set in a medium sized town based on Hines's native Barnsley, with its pit, its new estates surrounding the older town centre, and its rural areas on the outskirts of a 1960s estate. The main characters live on the council estate and the local pit is a major employer. There is also contact with the rural outskirts of the town, at Monastery Farm and Firs Hill, and with the town centre, though most of the action takes place on and around the estate where Billy Casper lives.

A good part of the novel is set in the secondary school which Billy Casper attends. Like most schools in the north of England in the 1960s, this was a secondary modern school. Comprehensive schools taking all abilities of pupils from a neighbourhood at eleven years old had begun to replace the selective system in the south of England, but did not reach many northern areas until well into the 1970s. At eleven years old, children sat the 'eleven plus' examination, with tests in reading comprehension, mathematics and verbal reasoning (often called an ' intelligence test'). The pupils who 'passed' the examination went to grammar schools, those who did not went to the local secondary modern. A smaller number went to technical schools where the curriculum was based on technology and pupils were trained to work in engineering or construction.

Secondary schools in the 1960s

At grammar schools, pupils followed an academic course and studied all subjects up to fourteen, and nine or ten subjects to GCE 'O' level, the equivalent of GCSE grades A* to C. At secondary modern schools in the 1960s, most pupils left at fifteen, the end of their fourth year. They left without taking any examinations. Their curriculum was less academic than at grammar schools and included English, mathematics, general science (but no physics, chemistry or biology); history, geography and practical subjects such as woodwork and metalwork for boys' schools and needlework and cookery for girls' schools. Games and PE were also included. Foreign languages were not usually studied. During the 1970s a new examination called CSE was introduced and the school-leaving age was raised to sixteen for all pupils so that everybody could take a school-leaving examination. CSE was equivalent to GCSE grades D to G, but there was a grade 1 which was supposed to be equal to a grade C. However, the secondary modern school in *A Kestrel for a Knave* had no school-leaving examination for most pupils (a few – the brightest – stayed on until sixteen at all secondary moderns and took 'O' levels). Most pupils left at fifteen and went straight into jobs.

While the grammar schools attracted the best qualified teachers and the most money for books and equipment, the secondary moderns had to make do with less money and less well qualified staff. There were some very good secondary modern teachers but many were like some of those Barry Hines portrays in the novel: uninterested in their pupils and there purely to earn a living. Secondary modern teachers were often considered to be of lower status, and many suffered from low morale. In addition, many pupils were anxious to leave school and start work as soon as possible and no doubt gave their teachers a hard time in the classroom! A class like 4C, Billy Casper's class, would not be easy to teach.

Work in the 1960s
When pupils left school, it was generally not too difficult to find work, as in the 1960s almost full employment existed. Many of the jobs the pupils went into would be unskilled work in factories, shops, and in general labouring, unless a boy wanted to train as an apprentice for a skilled trade such as bricklaying or electrical work. (It was far less common for girls to get apprenticeships and most girls from secondary modern schools worked in offices, shops or factories before

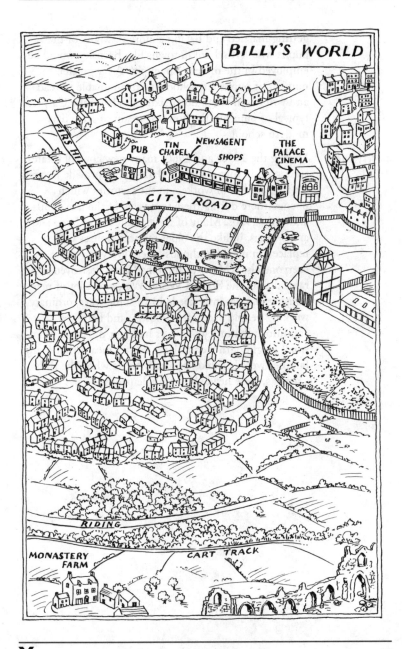

getting married and having children). Many of the
pupils who left school in towns like Barnsley would be
employed in the mine – 'down pit'. A far greater
number of pupils left school at fifteen unable to read
and write easily than do at sixteen today. Billy Casper is
typical of pupils in the bottom stream of secondary
modern school

Society and housing

During the 1950s and 1960s many new council estates
sprang up in towns such as Barnsley, to provide housing
for the families of workers in the factories which
opened there during the boom years of the late 1950s
and early 1960s. Many of these estates were large and
anonymous, unlike the older terraced houses they
replaced in neighbourhoods where everyone knew
everyone else. (Many of these had been destroyed in air
raids during the Second World War, and a lot of new
housing was urgently needed.) In some ways, ordinary
working people had better housing and better
conditions than they had ever had, but the move from
small neighbourhoods to large estates meant that many
families were isolated, especially those who, like Billy
Casper's, were headed by a single parent.

PART TWO

SUMMARIES

GENERAL SUMMARY

*Section 1
(pp. 7–44)
Billy's day
begins;
flashback to
getting Kes*

A Kestrel for a Knave depicts one day in the life of Billy Casper, a fifteen year old living in a northern town in the 1960s. There are several flashbacks (see Literary Terms) to other earlier parts of his life. We see his difficult home circumstances, his unsatisfactory experiences at school, and his love of animals and knowledge and expertise in training the kestrel hawk he calls Kes.

The novel opens with Billy Casper getting up early one morning when his elder brother Jud goes off to work down the local mine. There is no food in the house and Billy has to light the coal fire himself; his mother is still in bed. The reader sees Billy's morning routine, including his frustration when he has to walk his paper round because Jud has taken his bike. Billy is in trouble with his employer Mr Porter for this, but takes short cuts to finish his round on time. He steals orange juice and eggs from a milk dray on his route, and observes the very different lifestyles of some of the occupants of the houses up Firs Hill where he delivers papers. His mother has a series of boyfriends, one of whom, Reg, has stayed the night and is seen by Billy leaving the house. Billy refuses to go shopping for his mother on the grounds that she owes the local shopkeeper so much money that he has refused to let her have any more credit, and runs away when she pursues him, breaking the stolen eggs in the process. Before going to school he lets himself into a well cared for shed in the garden to look at Kes, his kestrel hawk, complaining to the bird that everyone is always after him.

A flashback (see Literary Terms) incident follows in which we learn how Billy discovered the kestrel's nest at Monastery Farm, tried to get a book from the local library on falconry in order to find out more about training kestrels, and stole one from a bookshop when refused entry to the library. When Jud came in drunk that night Billy fled the house, climbed the wall to the nest and selected a baby kestrel to bring home.

Section 2
(pp. 44–86)
Billy's school

The flashback ends abruptly when Billy realises the time and sets off for school, where we see some of the difficulties he has with teachers who are hostile to him. In trouble for a silly remark made during registration, he begins daydreaming about Kes in assembly and falls asleep on his feet, for which he is caned by Mr Gryce, the headmaster. He is caned along with Macdowall, accused of coughing in assembly; three boys who have been caught smoking; and a small boy sent with a message but ignored by Mr Gryce when he tries to explain. Afterwards he goes to his English lesson, where he is in trouble again for not listening, but makes up for it by giving the class a talk about Kes and how he trained her, though he has to be almost forced into doing this by Mr Farthing, his teacher. At break Billy becomes involved in a fight with Macdowall after Macdowall and others tease him about his mother's boyfriends and his difficult home life. Mr Farthing breaks it up and is sympathetic towards Billy, asking him if he can come and see Kes flying. Billy agrees.

Section 3
(pp. 86–126)
The games
lesson and
lunch-time

His next lesson is games with Mr Sugden, who dislikes Billy and angrily makes him wear an overlarge pair of shorts as a punishment for having no PE kit. Billy is forced to go in goal, which he hates, and is able to distract and lead away a large dog which is ruining the game even when everyone else is afraid. The game overruns the end of the lesson and Billy, who forgot to

swap sittings, realises that he is not going to get his
school dinner because he has to go home to feed Kes.
When he tries to get away quickly he is sent into the
showers by Mr Sugden, who then forces him to stand
underneath a cold shower as a punishment for letting
the last goal in.

Billy hurries home to feed Kes, only to find the money
for a bet which Jud has left, and which his mother has
already tried to insist he takes to the betting shop. He
shoots a sparrow to feed the hawk, and while he is
flying Kes free, Mr Farthing arrives to watch. The
teacher is admiring of Billy's skill and of the bird
herself, and offers Billy a lift back to school, which he
refuses because he has to take Jud's bet. Tempted to
spend the money on some dinner and cigarettes, he asks
at the betting shop whether the horses are likely to win.
The man he speaks to tells him that it is unlikely, so he
spends the money instead and returns to school for the
afternoon.

Section 4
(pp. 126–60)
Jud's revenge

When Jud arrives at school obviously looking for Billy,
it becomes evident that the horses have won and Billy is
in serious trouble. He avoids Jud by a series of
manoeuvres, ending up in the boiler-room where he
falls asleep for a while and misses his appointment with
the youth employment officer. When he tries to rejoin
his class unseen, Mr Gryce arrives and furiously sends
Billy along to keep his appointment.

Worried about what Jud may do, Billy cannot
concentrate when he sees the youth employment
officer, and apart from insisting that he will not work
down the mines, is not much help to him. When the
officer asks him about hobbies, he suddenly realises
what Jud might do and gets out of the room as quickly
as possible, running straight home. It is too late: the
shed is empty and the kestrel has gone.

Distraught, Billy runs the length and breadth of the locality looking for Kes even though he knows it is hopeless. When he fails to find the hawk he returns home to find his mother and Jud, who is furious because he would have won enough money to have a week off work if Billy had not kept the money for the bet. On hearing that Kes is in the dustbin, Billy rushes out and fetches the body, much to his mother's annoyance. It becomes obvious to Billy that his mother does not really understand how he feels and that she is powerless to punish Jud in any case, so he runs from the house and into the town centre, where he breaks into a disused cinema and sits alone in the darkness remembering a time when his father brought him there, and the events which led up to his father leaving home. He imagines himself and Kes up there on the screen starring in a film and triumphing over Jud, but eventually realises that in reality he can never beat Jud, so returns home to find no one in. The novel ends with his burying the hawk in the field behind his house, and going to bed.

DETAILED SUMMARIES

[SECTION 1]
(pp. 7–44)
Billy's day begins

On the first page we meet Billy Casper and his elder brother Jud, who works as a miner. Cramped housing forces the two to share a double bed. Jud gets up early to go to work, but makes sure he wakes Billy as he does, by refusing to reset the alarm or turn off the bedroom light. Jud reveals himself as a bully by thumping Billy when he awakes (see Commentary for character descriptions).

The paper round (p. 9)

Billy gets up, still in the dark, and finds a cold room and no food in the pantry. Jud has also taken all the milk so there is nothing for Billy's breakfast. He goes through his normal morning routine of lighting the fire, then just as he is about to set off for his paper round,

Look at the description of Billy lighting the fire on p. 9. Notice how the author begins to create a picture of his home life.

he discovers that Jud has taken his bike and is furious. He sets off for the newsagents, climbing the fence of the recreation ground to take a short cut. Mr Porter, his employer, is not pleased that Billy has to walk and tells him that there is a waiting list for his job. He is obviously suspicious of Billy especially as he comes from the council estate. While his back is turned Billy steals some chocolate from the counter.

Billy sets off on the paper round, up Firs Hill which is the wealthier district on the edge of town, with the moors and the countryside close by. He pauses while eating his chocolate to watch a thrush pull a worm from the ground, fascinated by bird life. When a milk dray appears on the road, he steals a bottle of orange juice and a carton of eggs as the driver delivers milk at nearby houses. The way in which he lingers to chat with and tease the driver shows how used to stealing he is.

Notice how the descriptions of the thrush on p. 13 and the house on p. 16 reveal things about Billy. Notice how the stone house contrasts with his home.

Up on the moors above the town, Billy stops to read a copy of *The Dandy* comic, turning to his favourite story 'Desperate Dan'. He delivers to a farm and then stops at a large stone house on his round, to look at the Bentley parked outside. While he is delivering the papers the owner comes out with his two daughters and Billy gets a glimpse of the inside of the house as he hands the newspaper to the man's wife.

When he returns to the paper shop, Billy meets more hostility from Mr Porter, who seems determined to criticise him. He gets his revenge by shaking the stepladder on which Porter is standing and then pretending to save him from falling. He goes home again, seeing his mother's latest boyfriend, Reg, leave the house just as he arrives. His mother seems annoyed when he questions her about Reg, asks Billy for a cigarette, then tells him to go to the local shop for some

Note how the exchange between Billy and his mother, on pp. 18 and 19, reveals their relationship and the kind of mother Mrs Casper is.

groceries as there is nothing in the house. When she tells him to ask for credit, Billy argues that the shopkeeper says that she cannot have anything else until her debts are paid. When he refuses to go, his mother swears at him, threatens him and tries to hit him, but he outmanoeuvres her and runs from the house leaving her sprawled on the floor. On the way out he arranges then breaks the eggs he has stolen from the milk dray. His mother appears, still threatening him and reminds him that there is a bet of Jud's for him to take. Billy says that he will not take it, and his mother hurries off to work saying 'Please yourself then'.

Billy goes to the shed to look at his hawk, Kes, before leaving for school. He stands talking to the bird, while he remembers the day he got the hawk the previous summer.

Flashback to last summer (p. 21)

A flashback to a day last summer now follows. Billy has got up early to go nesting with Tibbut and Macdowall, two of his school friends, and Jud is still having breakfast when he comes downstairs. It is a beautiful morning, but Jud points out to Billy that if he were going down the mine he would not be saying that. When Billy tells Jud that he will never work down the

*Look at the
conversation on
p. 22 between
Billy and Jud
to see if this is
typical of their
relationship.*

mines, Jud turns on him nastily and says that there is
no chance of his being taken on anyway. As Jud leaves
he forgets his snap (see Glossary) and Billy begins to
eat it, but Jud returns to snatch the remains from him.

When Billy reaches Tibbut's and Macdowall's houses
neither boy is up, and Mrs Macdowall tells him in no
uncertain terms to go away, so he ends up entering the
woods alone. The sun is just rising and it is a beautiful
morning. Billy stops frequently to admire features of
the natural world around him. In the woods he notes a
Scots pine with a nest near the top, and carefully
climbs up it, only to find the nest empty. He ends up in
the lane near Monastery Farm, where he spies a kestrel
hawk flying out of a nest in the wall of the old
monastery.

Billy, fascinated, watches the kestrel and its mate
transfer prey and the female hawk re-enter the nest to
feed her young. Eventually he falls asleep, tired by his
early start, and when he awakes it is the middle of the
day and a little girl, the farmer's daughter, is playing in
the monastery ruins near the farm. The farmer appears
and seems inclined to chase Billy away, but Billy
convinces him that he is genuinely interested in the
kestrels and the farmer allows him on the property to
watch the birds. He tells the farmer that he would like
to get a baby kestrel and train it. The farmer asks him
how he would do that, and advises him that he might
find out from a book on falconry.

Billy visits the City Library to borrow a book on
falconry, but the librarian is reluctant to let him in
because he is not a member. Billy is defeated by the
process of filling in a form, as he would have to wait
until the following Monday for his mother to sign it,
and so he leaves the library without a book. However,
he has asked the librarian where the nearest bookshop

Though a poor reader, Billy takes trouble to find and read the book on falconry, revealing much about his character.

is, and goes straight there, where he locates *A Falconer's Handbook*, and steals it when the shop assistants' backs are turned. It seems the easiest theft he has carried out.

When Billy arrives home and begins to read his book, Jud snatches it from him and throws it across the room, not understanding why Billy wants a book as he is a poor reader. Jud, as usual, bullies Billy into admitting why he wants the book and telling him his plans, then threatens him. He says that he will go round to the farm with a gun. At this point Mrs Casper comes in and tells Billy to get his own tea. She and Jud are both going out that Saturday night and discuss their plans. Neither of them listens to Billy nor shows any interest in his plans for preparing a nesting box in the shed and getting a kestrel to train. Mrs Casper gives Billy some money for crisps and lemonade and tells him not to be up when she comes in. Both Jud and Mrs Casper leave Billy struggling to read the falconry book.

Saturday night (p. 39)

It is a typical Saturday night in the Casper household, and Jud returns drunk. Billy is reading in bed, but at the sound of Jud's footsteps he feigns sleep. Jud stumbles drunkenly into the bedroom and demands loudly that Billy help him get undressed. Billy reluctantly complies, but complains how tired he is of this weekly routine. When Jud begins to snore it is too much for Billy and he begins to circle the bed, calling Jud a 'pig, hog, sow and drunken bastard'. Jud begins to wake and Billy, terrified of what he might do, runs from the house half dressed, out into the moonlit night.

Notice how the situation when Jud comes home tells us a lot about Billy's life.

Once out, Billy makes his way to the woods and Monastery Farm, making contact with an owl on the way and imitating its call until he gets it to answer him. At Monastery Farm he scales the monastery wall until he reaches the kestrels' nest. He feels into the nest and withdraws the baby kestrels one by one, until his jacket pocket is full of them. Gradually he selects the oldest,

most developed one and replaces the others carefully.
When he climbs down again with his chosen baby
kestrel his hands are scratched and bleeding but he is
happy, and hums to himself all the way home.

COMMENT We learn about Billy's home circumstances. His father
has left and his mother seems too busy with work and
her various boyfriends to take much notice of Billy. She
has no control over Jud, who bullies her as well as Billy,
and little control over Billy himself. As the novel
progresses, you will be able to guess that Billy is
powerless to protect himself against Jud's bullying, and
that this will have serious consequences for him.

Mrs Casper and Jud clearly get on much better than
Billy does with either of them; in one sense they are
two of a kind. They both put their own pleasure before
any responsibility, and seem to treat Billy as though he
were there just to run errands for them, when they are
not totally ignoring him. They appear to have little
family feeling either for each other or for Billy. Billy is
told to get his own tea, is sent to seek credit despite the
debts Mrs Casper has already run up, and is bought off
with money for lemonade and crisps as long as he is not
up when his mother returns, presumably with the
lastest boyfriend. Jud bullies Billy in a particularly
heartless way, which is not at all the usual bossiness of
an older brother towards a younger. It is rather a
deliberate physical and verbal attack on Billy at every
opportunity.

We also learn about Billy's character: he is a practised
thief and even has a pocket in his jacket especially for
hiding stolen goods. He steals from his employer, from
the milkman and from anywhere if he thinks he can get
away with it. He hates Jud, defies his mother and is
insolent to Mr Porter, his employer.

We also learn about another side to Billy: the nature

lover. He observes birds, animals and plants closely; knows a lot about their habitats, and spends a great deal of time and effort preparing for the arrival of his baby kestrel, even stealing a book though he finds reading difficult. He seems to lead a completely separate and different, purer existence outside his home. We see how important the kestrel is in his life. He talks to her rather than anyone in his family. Billy is a talented climber though as we see later his talents are not recognised in school games.

GLOSSARY

gi'o'er Yorkshire dialect (see Literary Terms): stop that, get off

thi'sen Yorkshire dialect: yourself

nog lump

owt Yorkshire dialect: anything

tab cigarette

shot spread light ammunition

nowt Yorkshire dialect: nothing

allus Yorkshire dialect: always

snap miner's lunch or snack

half-nelson forced position where the victim's arm is bent backwards

summat Yorkshire dialect: something

crabbing climbing technique for moving sideways across rock or steep wall

eyas a young fledgling kestrel hawk, which has not yet learned to fly

Identify the speaker.

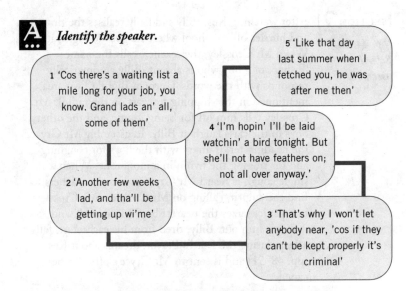

1 'Cos there's a waiting list a mile long for your job, you know. Grand lads an' all, some of them'

5 'Like that day last summer when I fetched you, he was after me then'

4 'I'm hopin' I'll be laid watchin' a bird tonight. But she'll not have feathers on; not all over anyway.'

2 'Another few weeks lad, and tha'll be getting up wi'me'

3 'That's why I won't let anybody near, 'cos if they can't be kept properly it's criminal'

Identify 'to what or whom' this comment refers.

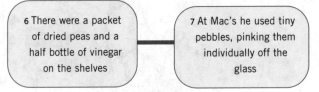

6 There were a packet of dried peas and a half bottle of vinegar on the shelves

7 At Mac's he used tiny pebbles, pinking them individually off the glass

Check your answers on page 80.

 Consider these issues.

a How the author creates the atmosphere (see Literary Terms) of Billy's home at the beginning of the novel.

b What Jud and Mrs Casper think of Billy and how they treat him.

c The different sides to Billy's character that we are shown.

d The advantages and disadvantages of telling the story from Billy's viewpoint.

e The author's use of Yorkshire dialect and frequent swearing; the effect this has on your impressions of the characters.

f How the author shows Billy's affection for Kes.

[SECTION 2]
(pp. 44–86)
School
assembly

After watching Kes, Billy suddenly realises the time and hurries off to school where he goes to registration. When Mr Crossley, the teacher, calls the name 'Fisher', of a boy who is absent, Billy automatically responds with the words 'German Bight' (Two areas mentioned in the shipping forecast on the radio). Mr Crossley tells him off for being idiotic, and the other boys in the class laugh at Billy. In assembly Mr Gryce, the headmaster, is angry with the boys for coughing and for singing the hymn in a monotone. When a single cough is heard Mr Gryce orders the teachers to find the culprit, calling on Mr Crossley. Mr Crossley, in a panic, seizes the nearest boy, Macdowall, and marches him out. Billy, tired from his early start, falls asleep during the Lord's Prayer, dreams about Kes (pp. 48–51) and is sent to Mr Gryce's office to be caned.

The caning
(p. 53)

Billy and Macdowall, who claims innocence, are joined by three smokers who have been caught by Mr Gryce. While they are waiting a small boy arrives with a message from a teacher, and joins the queue. The smokers force him to look after their cigarettes and lighters. Mr Gryce arrives, refuses to listen to anyone including the messenger, and lectures the boys about their bad behaviour before caning them. He claims that there has never been a younger generation as difficult to deal with as the present one, and contrasts their attitudes with those of previous generations who, as adults, will stop him in the street and laugh with him about the thrashings he once gave them. When he tells them to empty their pockets he finds the smoking equipment on the small boy and canes him as well. He does not give the boy a chance to explain and the younger child is too frightened of the older boys to say anything about where he got the cigarettes and lighters from.

The English lesson (p. 58)

Billy is late for his English lesson, where the teacher, Mr Farthing, is looking at differences between fact and fiction. Anderson, one boy in the class, tells an entertaining anecdote about his early life, when he and another boy filled his wellington boots with tadpoles and after being dared to put them on by the other boy, he stood in them. Mr Farthing picks Billy to follow this with a story but Billy, who has not been paying attention, is tongue-tied. Eventually, under a threat of class detention, Billy is persuaded to tell the class about Kes and how he trained her. He forgets his shyness and reluctance to join in as he becomes carried away with his story, and holds the class spellbound while he describes how he flew Kes free for the first time.

Notice how Billy does not tell the truth about where and how he got Kes.

By not commenting on Billy's 'tall story' the author creates a much more powerful effect.

After praising Billy for his talk, Mr Farthing sets the class to write a piece of fiction called 'A Tall Story'. Billy's tall story, which is badly spelled and hardly punctuated, tells of a typical day which he would like to have but knows is impossible. For many people, what he describes would be a normal day.

The fight (p. 73)

Break arrives, and Billy goes out into the yard where he is driven to the shelter of the cycle shed by the cold wind. Hanging round in the hope of a smoke are Macdowall and the three smokers whose cigarettes were

given to the messenger and then confiscated by
Mr Gryce. Macdowall begins to tease Billy, calling
him 'Casper the cadger' and threatening him. When
Billy walks away Macdowall follows him, playing to
his audience of other boys, and begins to make
remarks about Billy's mother and her many boyfriends.
Billy threatens to tell Jud, but Macdowall says that
Jud does not scare him and taunts Billy about Jud
not being his real brother, and about Billy's small
size.

*Notice how Mr
Farthing bullies
Macdowell.
Would a teacher be
allowed to do this
now?*

A rather unequal fight soon starts between Billy and
Macdowall, and draws a huge number of spectators.
Until Mr Farthing, on break duty, arrives and stops it.
Mr Farthing is impatient with both boys and tells them
off for the mess they have made of the coke in the shed,
but he is angrier with Macdowall for bullying someone
who is half his size. He pins Macdowall to the wall of
the shed and gives him a taste of what it is like to be
bullied by threatening him and using his physical size
to intimidate him. Macdowall is punished by having to
shovel the heap of coke back into place.

**Mr Farthing
talks to Billy**
(pp. 80–4)

Mr Farthing then turns to Billy and tries to find out
what happened from his point of view. He listens
sympathetically when Billy tells him about the reasons
he gets into trouble, and why he was caned that
morning. Though he laughs when Billy tells him about
the boy with the message being caned because Mr
Gryce would not listen to him, he agrees with Billy that
it is not funny. He asks about Billy's home life, and
tries to encourage him to look forward to work when he
leaves school. He also enquires whether Billy has been
in trouble with the police lately, and Billy tells him that
since he got Kes he has stopped getting into trouble,
and that this is one of the reasons why Macdowall and
his friends will not leave him alone. Eventually Mr
Farthing has to go and blow the whistle to end break,

but he arranges to come to Billy's home to see Kes before he goes.

We learn about the school and how Billy is treated by teachers.

Mr Farthing seems different from the rest of the teachers.

This conversation tells us a lot about both characters. We learn more about Billy's life and how hopeless he feels about school and his future.

Billy goes into the toilets to wash himself after the fight. There is a description of the typical messy school toilets, and of Billy daydreaming as he becomes fascinated by a bubble and puts off going to his games lesson, which he hates.

COMMENT

In this section we learn about Billy's life at school and also more about his character and his lack of hope for the future. The loneliness of a boy who listens to the shipping forecast every night comes across when he blurts out 'German Bight' in registration, and also the fact that he has few friends and is often the butt of the other boys' jokes.

Mr Gryce is portrayed as an unsympathetic and cold head teacher, out of touch with the young people in his charge and clearly tired of his job. The morning caning after assembly has become an unpleasant routine. He seems incapable of listening to the boys, as is shown when the poor messenger is caned because he has not been given a chance to explain. That this boy can end up in this situation, from a combination of bullying by the older smokers and Gryce's lack of understanding sums up the school's attitude to many of its pupils.

There is clearly tension between Billy and Macdowall. We learn that Billy has been in trouble with the police in the past, but that training Kes has given him an alternative interest. Macdowall and his former friends do not like the fact that Billy has stopped hanging round with them. Macdowall is a known troublemaker. When Mr Gryce demands that Mr Crossley catch the boy who coughed, Mr Crossley picks on Macdowall in panic and Gryce says, 'I might have known'. Mr Gryce puts unnecessary pressure on his staff in this incident, showing that he is as unsympathetic to them as he is towards the pupils. Billy teases Macdowall about bringing his father up to school, which leads to Macdowall's retaliation later on when he taunts Billy about his lack of a father. We learn that this is a particularly sore point with Billy as his father has left home and he misses him.

During the English lesson and the fight at break we see that Mr Farthing is different from the other teachers. He is interested in the boys, even prepared to visit them out of school, and he treats them as human beings rather than nuisances. He refuses to subside into the atmosphere of hopelessness which seems to affect the rest of the school and does his best, despite the limited ability of the boys, to make his lesson interesting. He does this by using the boys' own experiences and concentrating on oral work to prepare for the written task he sets, instead of simply using writing as a way of keeping them quiet and occupied. At first he is impatient with Billy because he refuses to join in, but gradually he coaxes him to tell his story and gives him the praise which is due. We feel that Billy's skill and patience have impressed the teacher and that he has learned something that day as well as the boys. He makes a genuine attempt to listen to Billy and understand the difficulties he faces, and he deals with Macdowall's bullying effectively, though not in a conventional way. (Nowadays a teacher would not be allowed to threaten a pupil physically.)

Billy's 'tall story' is in many ways the centrepiece of the novel. It depicts, in the poorly spelled and punctuated English of a boy of limited academic ability, a typical day in the life of many ordinary boys of Billy's age. Yet for him it is a 'tall story', and we are made poignantly aware of how Billy's life falls short of the normal standards most people expect from family life. The wishful thinking in the sentence about Jud going in to the army but Billy's dad coming back instead brings home to us how miserable Billy is without his father and how Jud makes his life so difficult. Even the meals are described, reminding the reader that in Billy's home there is rarely food in the pantry and all too often he is left to fend for himself.

GLOSSARY   **Fisher and German Bight** areas of sea mentioned in the Shipping Forecast on radio

gauntlet falconer's leather glove

mutes pieces of dung

jesses Small leather straps fastened around the legs of a trained hawk

bating hawk screaming in panic and trying to fly away

broddling Yorkshire dialect: searching about

prioll triple number card game

Missen Yorkshire dialect: myself

Bolus a large pill

the Bisto Kid character in 1960s' advertisement for Bisto Gravy mix

A *Identify the speaker.*

1 'And so did you, Casper. Just came out from under a stone'

2 'But what do I get from you lot? A honk from a greasy youth behind the wheel of some big second-hand car. Or an obscene remark from a gang – after they've passed me!'

5 'I've heard tha's got more uncles than any kid in this city'

4 'So you've to be right patient, an' all t'time you're walkin' her you've got to talk to her, all soft like, like you do to a baby'

3 'It was a funny feeling though when he'd gone; all quiet, with nobody there, and up to t'knees in tadpoles'

Identify the person 'to whom' this comment refers.

6 The boys stood looking up at Gryce, each one convinced that Gryce was looking at him

7 The first stroke made him cry. The second made him sick

Check your answers on page 80.

B *Consider these issues.*

a How the author creates the atmosphere of Billy's school in assembly and afterwards.

b What the caning incident tells you about Mr Gryce.

c How the author reveals more about different aspects of Billy's character.

d What you learn about Mr Farthing from
• the English lesson and
• his treatment of Billy and Macdowall after the fight.

[SECTION 3]

(pp. 86–126)
The games lesson

Note which side the author seems to be on when he describes this scene.

Billy now goes unwillingly to his much hated games lesson. Mr Sugden, the teacher is waiting for him. Mr Sugden thinks highly of himself and is smartly dressed in a violet track suit ready for a football match. He begins by accusing Billy of 'skiving' and makes sarcastic remarks to him when Billy explains that he has been talking to Mr Farthing. Billy explains that he has no PE kit and Sugden tells him loudly that he makes him sick. An argument develops with Sugden demanding to know why Billy cannot get any kit and Billy answering back. Eventually the teacher throws a huge, oversized pair of shorts at Billy and tells him to put them on. As Billy protests and Sugden shouts orders we sense that this sort of scene happens every games lesson.

The class goes out on to the field and Sugden orders Tibbut to pick a team while he picks another. Of course despite Tibbut's protests the teacher has first pick. The other boys are forced to line up and be chosen in order. No one wants Billy. He is left until last, along with the other misfits in the class: fat boys who cannot run fast, a boy with spots, one with a hare lip and one with glasses. After an argument over which end to play, and having laid down the law as to who are the best national footballers, Sugden realises that there is no one in goal. Despite his protests, Billy is chosen to play goalie.

When the game begins it is obvious that Sugden, while he fancies himself as a football star, is a clumsy and inept player, but he forces his way through the boys and cheats when their skill is greater than his.

Billy makes no attempt to save the goal that is scored, and in revenge Sugden throws the muddy ball at him so hard that he falls over and is covered in mud.

*See how much you
can learn here
from Sugden's
reaction.*

The game continues among complaints from Mr Sugden's team about his lack of skill. Billy meanwhile has become bored and is playing with the wire-netting pretending to be a lion. He then climbs the post and begins swinging on the cross-bar. Billy shows some ability at gymnastics here but like a lot of his behaviour at school, it is misplaced.

The game continues, with each team scoring a goal. Billy is unable to save one, and the other, scored by Sugden's team to equalise, appears to be from an offside position.

A large mongrel dog now appears on the field, barking and taking the ball. All the boys, and Mr Sugden, are scared and get away from the ball quickly. Only Billy is calm. Sugden orders Billy to get half a dozen cricket bats from the games store in order to move the dog but Billy quickly calms the animal down and walks it quietly off the field. Each team scores one more goal and Sugden announces that the next one will decide the match. By now Billy and many of the other boys are cold and tired and want the game to end especially as it is lunch-time.

Mr Sugden refuses to end the lesson until a winning goal has been scored. Billy protests that he is on first sitting for dinner but gets no sympathy from Sugden, who tells him to forget about his meal. But Billy says to anyone who will listen that he has to go home at lunch-times to feed his hawk.

Eventually, Billy pretends to save a goal but lets it in, and the boys immediately abandon the pitch and rush inside.

The shower (p. 103)

Mr Sugden stops Billy just as he is setting off home and demands to know whether he has had a shower, knowing well that he has not. When Billy tries to lie Sugden hits him and orders him to undress and shower. As soon as Billy is under the shower Mr Sugden turns the water temperature from hot to cold, and forces Billy to stand under the freezing water by posting three boys as guards at the end. When Billy protests, Mr Sugden replies that it was not fair when Billy let in the last goal. Billy tries to dodge but in the end gives up and just stands under the cold water spray. Eventually Billy manages to escape over the partition wall separating the showers from the changing rooms, and immediately dresses to rush off home.

Observe how Sugden's character is revealed by his behaviour towards Billy in the shower.

Lunch-time (p. 108)

Loading his rifle with pellets to shoot a sparrow for the hawk's dinner, he notices two coins and a slip of paper from Jud: instructions about a bet. He decides to let a shot at one of the coins decide whether he takes the bet or not, but the shot goes against him. Swearing, he pockets the money and paper.

Outside Billy shoots a sparrow to feed Kes, and takes her outside to fly her to the lure. Just as he is getting started Mr Farthing arrives to watch. He gives Mr Farthing a fine demonstration of his skills as he flies the hawk, luring her on until he ends the performance

(pp. 86–126)

Look again at Billy's conversation with Mr Farthing on pp. 116–19. Notice what this shows about their relationship now that Mr Farthing has watched Billy with Kes.

by letting the hawk take the meat. Mr Farthing is suitably impressed and tells Billy how brilliant he is, while they watch Kes eat the sparrow. They then return to the shed to talk about Kes and Billy's attitudes to wildlife in general. Billy's conversation with Mr Farthing is unlike those he has had with any teacher in the school

Mr Farthing offers Billy a lift back to school but Billy refuses, embarrassed as he has to visit the betting shop first. He delays going after Mr Farthing has driven off, playing instead with the tiny skull and bones excreted by the hawk. Eventually he makes his way to the betting shop, but is distracted by the smell of fish and chips from down the street. Again he tosses a coin to decide whether or not to take the bet, and when the toss goes against him decides on the best of three. However, he still loses.

Billy enters the betting shop and looks around for advice. He approaches a man at the table and asks him whether the horses are likely to win. The reply indicates that if they do, Jud will win quite a lot, as he has got them doubled, but that it is unlikely. This is exactly what Billy wants to hear. He immediately throws the slip of paper into the fireplace, where it bounces off without catching fire, and goes to the fish and chip shop to buy some dinner. He then visits the butcher's van for some beef, and as the butcher lets him have a scrap free, buys ten cigarettes and a box of matches with the remaining money. He walks back to school eating his fish and chips.

Billy was unwise to spend the money. What may happen now?

COMMENT   In this section we learn more about Billy's school life, especially his relationship with the games teacher Mr Sugden, and about Sugden as a character. The football match provides much humour, but also a bleak commentary on Billy's experience of school, and an insight into how teachers like Sugden ignore some of

Billy's abilities: his athletic skill, for example, and his skill with animals when he is able to persuade the large dog to leave the field with him.

The incident in the showers shows the general lack of sympathy for Billy among the other pupils, but it also shows the sadistic side of the teacher and the way in which he gets away with treating an unpopular pupil in this cruel way.

In complete contrast, Mr Farthing's coming to Billy's home to watch him fly Kes shows his genuine interest in Billy as a person and his appreciation of Billy's talent. Farthing speaks to Billy as an equal, never talking down to him during the conversation they have in the shed. However it is obvious that Billy is embarrassed by the fact that he is offered a lift back to school because he has to go to the betting shop for Jud. There is a huge gulf between their worlds.

His decision to spend the betting money on fish and chips is understandable in the light of the events of lunch-time, since Sugden has forced him to miss his dinner and he has had no proper breakfast either. Does this make it right?

GLOSSARY   **knackered** (colloquial) tired out, useless

Thalidomide drug, given in the 1950s and 1960s to pregnant women, which caused deformities in babies including lack of arms and/or legs

Eros Greek god of love, often depicted as a small naked boy in statues and paintings

chassé dance movement where two partners reverse positions

the final solution refers to the Nazi extermination of 6 million Jews during the Second World War. Billy running towards the showers is compared in his thinness and dirty appearance to the many children who were killed after being imprisoned in dreadful conditions

feake wipe beak after feeding

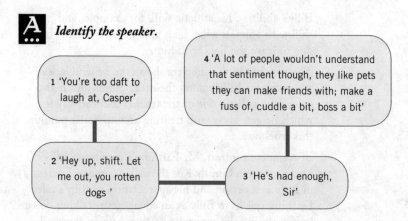

A ... Identify the speaker.

1 'You're too daft to laugh at, Casper'

4 'A lot of people wouldn't understand that sentiment though, they like pets they can make friends with; make a fuss of, cuddle a bit, boss a bit'

2 'Hey up, shift. Let me out, you rotten dogs '

3 'He's had enough, Sir'

Identify the person 'to whom' this comment refers.

5 His disappointed Forwards muttered amongst themselves as they trooped back out of the penalty area

7 With his overcoat on, and his trousers pinched up, he looked like a day tripper paddling at the seaside

6 He resembled an old print of a child hurrying towards the final solution

Check your answers on page 80.

B ... Consider these issues.

a How the author creates an amusing picture of Mr Sugden in this part of the novel.

b What more we learn about Billy from the games lesson and what happens at lunch-time.

c How Mr Sugden treats Billy. Does this alter your impression of him?

d Mr Farthing's response to seeing Billy fly Kes.

e What leads up to Billy deciding not to take Jud's bet.

f How the author creates a sense that things will go horribly wrong for Billy.

[SECTION 4]
(pp. 126–60)
Jud's revenge

Note how this description prepares us for the outcome.

Having finished his fish and chips bought with Jud's betting money, Billy returns to school for the afternoon. The section begins with a description of the atmosphere in the school on a dark and threatening afternoon. Billy is in a mathematics lesson, almost falling asleep, when the teacher sees him and shouts at him to get on with his work. Startled, Billy wakes up but is soon almost asleep again. As he dozes, Jud walks slowly past the school looking into all the rooms, then turns in up the drive. The window is too steamed up for Billy to see properly what has happened, but he is aware that someone has just come up the drive and a horrible realisation begins to dawn on him. He tries to ask others in the class whether they have just seen who it was, but just then Jud's steel-tipped heels are heard in the corridor outside the room. Colour drains from Billy's face as the class watches his reaction to Jud's appearance at the window in the classroom door. The teacher, noticing his pallor, asks him if he feels sick and would he like to go outside for a drink of water, which of course is the last thing Billy wants! The bell goes for the end of the lesson, and however slowly Billy tries to move, the books are collected in and the class dismissed all too quickly. When he follows the teacher out of the room, there is Jud talking to Tibbut further down the corridor.

Billy runs for cover (p. 130)

He stays with the teacher until he enters another classroom, then sprints away before Jud can catch him. Hiding in the toilets, he realises that the air brake slowly shutting the door will give him away, and rushes out into the yard. As Jud enters the toilets and begins to bang each cubicle door back with his boots, Billy runs, hunched down, along the wall under the classroom windows. He runs into the cloakroom where he hides among a pile of coats.

Back into the toilets and out into the yard again, Billy

manages to stay one step ahead of Jud, and eventually seeks sanctuary in the boiler-room as the door is open. Before long he is asleep.

When he wakes up the caretaker has returned and the light is on, but he has only come for his cigarettes and leaves without seeing Billy. Billy now judges it is safe to leave, so he rushes across the playground into the school building and finds his class again. Tibbut tells him that everyone, including Mr Gryce, has been looking for him during the last lesson, as he should have gone for his interview with the youth employment officer. Billy has forgotten all about this. Gryce is waiting for Billy at the next classroom door and boxes his ears, sending him off to the interview with expressions of despair. As Billy dodges being hit by Mr Gryce, a small boy who is walking on the wrong side of the corridor is cuffed across the ear by the headmaster instead.

Notice how Mr Gryce treats all the pupils, even the small boy.

Billy waits outside the medical room, where the interviews are held, with another boy who has his mother with him. Of course Mrs Casper is not there.

The youth employment officer (p. 135)

Eventually the interview ends and Billy makes no attempt to go in, having to be called in by the youth employment officer. Billy is unhelpful to the officer, simply saying that he has not thought about what he wants to do. The officer finds no help in his records either, and the only thing they seem to be able to establish is that Billy has difficulty reading and writing. The officer writes 'Manual' on his records and begins his prepared speech about trades, apprenticeships and studying for exams at technical college, right up to degree level. Most of this is irrelevant to Billy, who does not appear to be listening. Nearing the end of his speech, the youth employment officer recommends mining, and here Billy suddenly comes to life for the

How much is the youth employment officer really helping Billy?

first time in the interview, declaring that he will not go 'down pit'. Nonplussed, the officer turns to hobbies, asking what Billy's interests are.

His question seems to remind Billy of something. He stands up and asks if he can go, but the officer has not finished yet and detains him. He finishes filling in his records and gives him the relevant leaflet on leaving school, and getting insurance cards.

Billy searches for Kes (p. 140)

As soon as he can escape, Billy runs straight out of school and home, but he is too late. The shed is empty and the hawk has gone. The door has been forced open. When he runs into the house there is no one there.

Think about whether Billy really expects to find Kes.

Devastated, Billy runs outside into the rain, and searches for Kes, patrolling the fields at the back of the house, swinging the lure and calling to the hawk continuously. Eventually he runs into the street, where he surprises a neighbour by darting out in front of a car and asking her if she has seen Jud.

Billy's next stop is the bookmaker's shop, where he meets Mrs Rose who tells him what has happened when Jud found out that the horses had won. Jud has wreaked havoc in the betting shop and threatened people with violence. Still more distressed, Billy returns to the fields and begins calling for Kes even though he senses it is hopeless. He covers all the ground where he has trained and flown the hawk: the fields, the hedgerows, the woods where he went nesting, and ends up at Monastery Farm. Here the wall in which the kestrels had nested has been torn down. Billy stands staring at where the wall has been, then finally, defeated, makes his way back to the estate and his house.

The family row (p. 147)

This time the light is on and Jud and Mrs Casper are at the tea table. Startled by the clatter of his entrance, they sit down again when they see who it is, and Billy's

mother completely fails to notice how upset he is.
When Billy repeatedly asks Jud where Kes is, Jud
ignores him. Eventually there is a shouting match and
when she finds out that Billy has kept the money rather
than put the bet on for Jud, Mrs Casper is more

Consider whether
Billy's mother can
really cope with
his distress.

sympathetic to Jud than Billy. Billy demands to know
whether Jud has killed the hawk because he could not
catch him, and Jud says that he has. Billy's attempt to
get sympathy from his mother by burying his face in
her only seems to embarrass her. Jud tells Billy that the
hawk is in the bin, so he rushes outside to get the body.
He returns to the kitchen, trying desperately to shock
his mother into doing something to punish Jud by
showing her the body, but she is clearly out of her
depth in this situation and tells him to take it away
from the table. Billy realises that his mother is
powerless to punish Jud in any way, and she loses her
patience with Billy, telling him that Kes is only a bird
and he can get another.

Beside himself with grief and anger, Billy knocks hot
tea over Jud, leaps on him, and when tackled by his
mother, kicks out at her also. Using the body of Kes to
fend them off, he dodges both Jud and Mrs Casper and
races from the house, banging both doors. The noise of
the screaming and fighting, in which furniture has
been knocked over, has brought the neighbours to their
front doors. They watch as Mrs Casper chases Billy and
calls to him to come back, and as he runs off into the
night.

Billy mourns
his loss
(p. 153)

Billy slowly calms down as he walks along the road and
realises that he is still clutching the hawk's body. He
puts it into his jacket pocket and continues along the
road. He passes the houses of most of the people he
knows as he wanders aimlessly around the estate.

Billy comes out on to the City Road, and lingers by a
derelict cinema, the Palace. He inspects the locked

gates and the delapidated front, then breaks in
through the boarded-up toilet window at the side.
Making himself a torch with a roll of newspaper, Billy
wanders through the old cinema. In the auditorium he
finds the seats and the carpet have been removed, so he
walks down to where a few of the old plush seats have
been stacked at one side, takes one of the cushions to
the back of the stalls, and sits down on it, letting the
newspaper torch burn out. As he sits in the darkness
he recalls an earlier time when his father brought him
here, when it was still open for business.

Flashback to Billy's dad (p. 158)

In a flashback (see Literary Terms) scene Billy recalls
seeing the Big Picture with his dad, a warm, cosy and
pleasant experience, then returning home to find his
'Uncle Mick' in the house. This was clearly one of his
mother's boyfriends, and Jud was in his car seated at
the wheel. He recalls his mother and Uncle Mick
leaping up off the settee when his father entered and
turned on the light, and the fight that followed before
Uncle Mick left with a cut under his eye. He recalls the
argument and shouting that followed between his
parents, and then his father packing a case and leaving
for good.

Think why Billy breaks into the disused cinema.

(pp. 126–60)

Billy's
daydream
(p. 159)

Billy drifts into a daydream of starring in a film on the cinema screen with Kes, of casting her off and her attacking Jud as he runs away. Abruptly he seems to become aware of where he is, and blunders out of the stalls, through the foyer and back into the toilet, where he climbs out of the window through which he entered the cinema. He shudders as though someone is walking over his grave as he turns away from the building and stands on the pavement.

Finally Billy turns round and walks back home. When he arrives there is no one in. He buries Kes in the fields just behind the shed she lived in, then goes in and goes to bed.

COMMENT

Look at the
language used to
do this.

This last part of the novel shows Jud's revenge on Billy and we can see as soon as he spends the bet money that it will end in disaster. The ominous description of the weather and the atmosphere (see Literary Terms) in the mathematics lesson help to prepare us for this.

When Jud arrives at school looking for Billy, the author creates a sense of his increasing panic as he hides from Jud.

Billy does not get very much out of his youth employment interview. Some of this is his fault and some is the interviewer's. It is interesting to examine who is more at fault and whether the interviewer really tries to give Billy good careers advice.

When Billy discovers Kes in the bin, his mother fails to understand how he feels. Try to examine whether it is because she is on Jud's side or whether she is incapable of sympathising with anyone but herself?

When Billy, in his desperate search for Kes, ends up at Monastery Farm, we learn that the wall has been torn down and the nest has gone, which means that Billy will not be able to get another kestrel to replace Kes.

The flashback (see Literary Terms) the old cinema gives us more background information about Billy's earlier life, and helps to explain the person he has become.

The ending is sad and stark. Think about why the author has chosen to end the novel in this way.

GLOSSARY   **Yale** type of lock easily opened from inside though not from outside. Billy smiles because he would otherwise be locked in the boiler-room where he has hidden from Jud

your cards National Insurance Cards. During the 1960s when the novel was written, these cards were required by anyone starting work. They contained a record of National Insurance contributions paid by employees. Someone who left a job would be given their cards to take on to the next employer. Hence the saying 'To get your cards' which meant to get the sack from a job

welcher a cheat, someone who goes back on their word

A *Identify the speaker.*

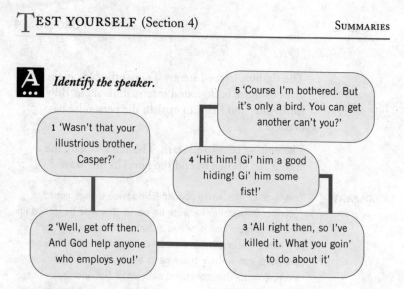

1 'Wasn't that your illustrious brother, Casper?'

5 'Course I'm bothered. But it's only a bird. You can get another can't you?'

4 'Hit him! Gi' him a good hiding! Gi' him some fist!'

2 'Well, get off then. And God help anyone who employs you!'

3 'All right then, so I've killed it. What you goin' to do about it'

Identify the person 'to whom' this comment refers.

6 'I wouldn't have thought he was the type to pay his old school a visit?'

8 'Called me all t'names under t'sun. Called me a welcher, and said I was trying to rob his eyes out'

7 'There doesn't seem to be a job in England to suit you'

Check your answers on page 80.

B *Consider these issues.*

a How the author conveys Billy's sense of panic when Jud arrives at the school.

b Whether Billy does the right thing when he runs from Jud and hides. Could he have saved Kes from being killed if he had stayed where he was?

c Mrs Casper's attitudes to Billy and to Jud after Kes is killed.

d What we learn about Billy's earlier life from the flashback in the cinema.

e What this flashback tells us about Mrs Casper.

f What Billy is feeling at the end of the novel and what might happen to him now.

PART THREE

COMMENTARY

THEMES

The main themes in *A Kestrel for a Knave* focus on
people and environment, and their effects on each
other, and in particular the effects of family
breakdown; and the experience of school. Billy, the
central character, is affected by his family and home
situation including the town and the estate where he
lives. School has an important if negative effect on
his life, while the natural world and wild life are an
opposing and positive influence on him, and perhaps
the one aspect of his life which saves him from
despair.

THE PHYSICAL ENVIRONMENT

Billy lives in a mining town where the 'pit' is a major
employer: the youth employment officer recommends
mining to all male school leavers lacking academic
ability or qualifications. He does not live in the town
centre but on a large council estate on the outskirts, as
close to the surrounding countryside and moors as to
the town itself. The position of the estate is important
in allowing Billy to develop his interest in wildlife and
the natural world because he is near enough to the edge
of the town to escape to the moors and the land and
woods around Monastery Farm, where the kestrel's nest
is found.

There is much description of the natural world and the
countryside close to Billy's home: e.g.
 • The thrush pulling a worm from the ground is
   described in detail.
 • The wood where Billy goes nesting is vividly
   described, including the discovery of a thrushes' nest.

'An Eagle for an Emperor ... a Kestrel for a Knave'.

- The kestrels transferring prey are described as Billy watches them, fascinated.
- The contrasting description of the route through the woods to Monastery Farm by moonlight sets the scene for Billy's bringing Kes home.
- Anderson's story about the tadpoles in the English lesson indicates a childhood linked to the natural world.
- There are passages describing Billy's training and flying of Kes in which each movement is depicted in vivid detail.

See Language & Style for further details.

The picture built up of the estate and town shows evidence of vandalism and people's lack of care for their environment. A particular example is the description of the area round the betting shop, where holes have been made in the fences and the earth is like ' a snotty sleeve'. There is also the example of the damage done to the tiles in the school by sliding in studded football boots.

Billy's character changes when surrounded by the natural world.

All these descriptive passages emphasise the effect that both the natural world and the built up environment have on Billy and other characters in the novel. Billy is between them both. He is a more positive, involved and skilled person when he is handling Kes, walking in the woods, or climbing trees and the monastery wall. At school and on the estate he is a vandal, a thief and a rogue. Other member of the Casper family, Mrs Casper and Jud, have no contact with the natural world and seem poorer for it. It is significant that the one thing Billy is determined not to do is to work down the mine. Symbolically, this would cut him off from the natural world.

ANIMALS

Animals as part of the natural world are an important theme in *A Kestrel for a Knave*. The book opens with a quotation from the *Boke of St Albans*, and assigns different birds of prey to men of various statuses. The emperor, at the top of the hierarchy, gets the most regal and powerful of all birds of prey, an eagle. The knave, at the bottom of the hierarchy, and a villain as well, gets a kestrel. This is the clue to the novel's title and subject-matter: the kestrel is an appropriate bird for Billy Casper because he is a 'knave' in both the fifteenth-century sense of the word (meaning at the bottom of the social and economic hierarchy) and in the twentieth-century sense of being a rogue or a thief.

As well as Kes, other animals are important to the theme of nature as a healing force and a good influence on Billy and other characters. During Billy's paper round he watches a thrush closely. He is described as stroking baby thrushes during his nesting expedition, and when he returns to Monastery Farm at night he maintained contact with an owl by imitating its call. He is generally more at home with birds and animals than he is with his family or school mates. It is significant that the ferocious looking mongrel who appears on the football field during Mr Sugden's lesson responds only to Billy, docilely allowing him to lead it off the field and away from the ball. During the English lesson, which is the only time when Billy's home and school life seem to meet at all, Anderson's story about the tadpoles reminds the reader that animals play an important part in the childhood of many of the boys. There is a sense of many of the characters having lost touch with the natural world as they are only ever described in terms of city life or life on a housing estate or drab school, but Billy remains between both worlds.

LACK OF FAMILY LIFE

The Caspers' home life is vividly depicted. There seems to be no support for the Casper family from their neighbours, who only appear on their doorsteps when there is a major row. There seems to be no sense of community on the estate, with everyone making their own holes in fences to take short cuts, parking their cars over the disks warning them to keep off seeded verges, and generally vandalising their environment.

Within the Casper household, Billy's surroundings are bleak. The house is poorly furnished and the family ill provided for. Billy has to share a bed with Jud, and they have no curtains in their bedroom. He finds no food in the pantry when he gets up in the morning. The family appears to have no sense of personal ownership: Jud puts Billy's jumper on in the morning as a vest, while Billy in turn wears his mother's sweater in order to keep warm while he is delivering papers. In general the family clothes seem poor. Billy has a jacket with a broken zip and plimsolls which leak, while his mother's shoes are worn and in need of a polish. Mrs Casper has refused for years to buy Billy the appropriate PE kit for school.

Billy's mother is totally self-centred.

There is a general lack of care, both physical and emotional, in the home environment. Mrs Casper does not get tea for Billy when he arrives home – she tells him to get his own; and when he bursts in on the night Jud has killed Kes, she is unconcerned once she sees who it is, and fails to notice his agitation. She goes out on a Saturday night leaving Billy in on his own, and her main concern is that he is not still up when she comes in, as she wishes to bring one of her boyfriends back to the house. Indeed, Mrs Casper's boyfriends are the talk of school where Macdowall uses her relationships to taunt Billy about having more 'uncles' than any other boy in the city. Mrs Casper has very little control over Billy, who comes and goes as he pleases and has been in trouble with the police for breaking and entering. It is only his training of Kes, which leaves him no time to hang about with Macdowall and his gang, which stops Billy from getting into trouble with the law.

Family breakdown Family breakdown is an important theme, in particular the effect on Billy of his father's departure. We do not find out why Billy's father left until almost the end, though Mrs Casper's behaviour with her male friends gives us a strong clue. The scene where Billy breaks into the Palace cinema, now disused, and remembers the time when he was there with his father and they returned home to catch Mrs Casper on the sofa with 'uncle' Mick explains the father's reason for leaving and Billy's heartbreak. The departure of the father seems to have led to Mrs Casper losing any sort of control over Jud, who from the moment his father left seems to have bullied Billy unmercifully.

THE EXPERIENCE OF SCHOOL

Billy's home environment is bleak, his experiences at school are not much better. School and its effect on its pupils are an important theme in *A Kestrel for a Knave*.

From the moment Billy arrives at school he is bullied by teachers and pupils alike. Barry Hines seems intent on showing that in the secondary modern school Billy attends, much of the bullying in fact comes from the teachers. Teachers such as Mr Crossley, who make brief appearances at registration and assembly, and the mathematics teacher who is not even named, treat Billy and the others boys with disinterest, even contempt. Mr Crossley thinks nothing of making a fool of Billy in front of the class and is overtly insulting to him. The maths teacher makes disparaging references to Jud, fails to notice the source of Billy's fear and agitation and in the end totally ignores him.

With the exception of Mr Farthing, the teachers with whom Billy is shown having closer contact in his school day treat him equally badly. Mr Gryce dislikes children, is totally unsympathetic, highly concerned with appearances and seems almost to enjoy caning the boys, though he makes a great show of complaining about having a line of boys outside his room each morning for the cane. The caning of the messenger indicates an almost total lack of understanding from an experienced teacher of the ways of boys; most heads would be aware that the large number of cigarettes and lighters could not possibly belong to one small boy and would have heard what he said about bringing a message from Mr Crossley.

Think how Barry Hines uses the messenger boy to make his point.

Mr Sugden also shows a dislike of Billy in particular and boys who do not like games in general. Even for those who do like football, the match brings little joy, as the teacher is intent on showing off his own prowess rather than teaching the pupils to improve their footballing skills.

In general, the teachers at the school do not seem to like nor wish to teach the boys. They are depicted by the author as time-servers, always looking at their watches to see how long it is until the end of the lesson, and having no interest in the boys as people. Many teachers find the mistakes pupils sometimes make amusing and can laugh with rather than at them, not so these teachers.

Lessons and teaching methods

Teaching methods seem old-fashioned by today's standards: in the mathematics lesson the boys are left to get on with a series of exercises without any help, while the teacher reads a book and insists on silence. He only looks up from his book to shout at any boy who does not appear to be concentrating. In games, football is played but skills are not practised, nor are boys given a chance to try different positions and gain different skills. Billy goes in goal because no one else wants to and he is unpopular. There is no thought given to the feelings of less popular boys or those who are not good at games. This is shown in particular in the practice of the teacher letting one of the more able footballers, Tibbut, pick one team while he himself selects another, and the rest of the boys have to line up. Of course the least popular and least sporty boys are chosen last every week, and have to suffer the indignity of waiting until last while everyone else has been chosen.

The teacher who is the exception to all this is Mr Farthing. He tries to involve the boys. His lesson on Fact and Fiction may still seem old-fashioned by modern standards, but he

- uses talk and the boys' own experiences
- seems genuinely interested in listening to them and encourages them to listen to each other
- does not insist on a silent writing task to keep them busy, while he marks or reads
- uses humour and is not afraid to enjoy a joke with his class

Outside class: other aspects of school

Outside class, school is not much better for Billy nor for any boy who is weaker or less popular than the majority. Bullying, both verbal and physical, is common and unless a fight actually breaks out, you feel that the teachers would neither discover nor tackle the problem. The playground environment is harsh, noisy and unwelcoming, with the hard asphalt surface and the dingy bike sheds behind which the smokers and the bullies hang about. The physical environment has few comforts for teachers or boys and the school lavatories, which get a page of description of their own, are typical of the bleak environment in which all the boys exist.

STRUCTURE

A single day   The structure of this novel is not strictly chronological. It is written so that it presents Billy Casper's life and the problems and issues he faces within a single day, starting with his waking in the early morning and ending with his going to bed at night. It is in the form of an episodic narrative with some flashbacks (see Literary Terms) depicting earlier parts of Billy Casper's life.

The beginning and ending of the novel, in the bleak bedroom he shares with Jud, remind us of the inadequacies of Billy's home life and his environment, in a neatly circular manner, bringing us back to the beginning and making us realise that for Billy things do not get any better as the novel progresses. In fact there is no progress for Billy. He is making the transition from school to working life, but there is no indication that he will enjoy work any more than school, as he tells Mr Farthing at the centre of the novel. Also, by the end he has lost Kes, with no chance of a replacement, and we are left with a sense of hopelessness as the final sentence of the novel shows him burying the hawk which has been at the centre of his experiences throughout.

Think how the author uses Kes to tell us about Billy and his future.

Within the structural confines of the one day in Billy's life, the author faces a problem: how to tell the reader about past events, and how to range more widely over the circumstances of Billy Casper's life and the environment in which he lives. He does this by the use of flashback.

Flashbacks   Flashback as a technique was becoming popular in the 1960s when this novel was written, probably because of the popularity of film and television. The technique of suddenly jumping back to an earlier period in the life of the main character was borrowed from the moving image of film and television. It helps an author who wishes to structure a novel in the present, as Barry

Y

Hines does, to show the reader a wider range of the character's experiences.

The first flashback in the novel occurs about thirteen pages into the narrative, after Billy and his family have been introduced, and Billy has gone through his usual morning routine, through which we learn about his life and his home environment. The flashback is to the morning he went nesting, alone, because both Tibbut and Macdowall failed to turn up as arranged. This flashback also mirrors the structure and form of the main narrative, in that it deals with a day in Billy's past, starting with the nesting in the early morning, complete with descriptive passages showing Billy's love of nature and the importance of the environment to him. The day progresses with his watching the kestrels, talking to the farmer, and then attempting to borrow a book on falconry from the local library and stealing when his intentions are thwarted by the librarian. When he reaches home, there is more detail about his home life and the relationships between Billy, Jud and Mrs Casper as the older two prepare for their Saturday night out. The day ends with Jud coming in drunk, waking up Billy, and Billy's reaction to him, and the flashback ends with an account of Billy's fleeing the bedroom and climbing the monastery wall to take a baby kestrel from the nest.

Notice how the flashback is like a kind of escape from everyday life.

The end of this first flashback brings us neatly to Billy in the present, looking at Kes on his way to school, and leads into the narrative which is concerned with his school day and his experiences of education.

A second, shorter piece of flashback occurs when Billy is daydreaming during the Lord's Prayer in assembly, and tells the reader more about how he trained or manned Kes and his relationship with the hawk.

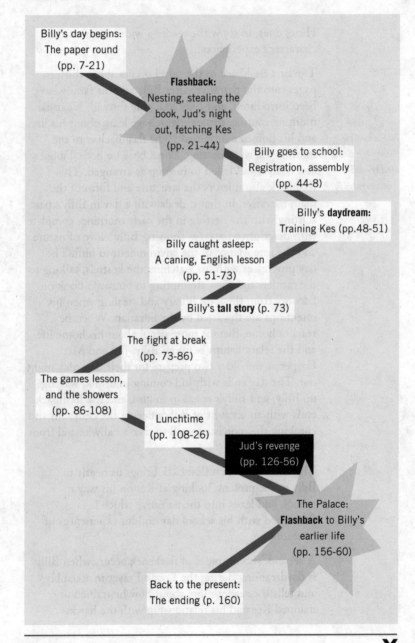

Billy's day begins:
The paper round
(pp. 7-21)

Flashback:
Nesting, stealing the
book, Jud's night
out, fetching Kes
(pp. 21-44)

Billy goes to school:
Registration, assembly
(pp. 44-8)

Billy's **daydream:**
Training Kes (pp.48-51)

Billy caught asleep:
A caning, English lesson
(pp. 51-73)

Billy's **tall story** (p. 73)

The fight at break
(pp. 73-86)

The games lesson,
and the showers
(pp. 86-108)

Lunchtime
(pp. 108-26)

Jud's revenge
(pp. 126-56)

The Palace:
Flashback to Billy's
earlier life
(pp. 156-60)

Back to the present:
The ending (p. 160)

The English lesson	The third revelation of Billy's past and his relationship with Kes comes in the English lesson when he tells the story to the class. This is part of the author's technique in showing how he overcomes his academic and personal limitations to show his expertise which neither his classmates nor his teacher have ever suspected before.
Chronological narrative	The next parts of the narrative, which deal with the fight and bullying at break, the conversation with Mr Farthing, the games lesson and the incident in the showers, the events of lunch-time and the afternoon at school, are purely chronological, until Billy runs home and discovers Kes missing, searches vainly for her and confronts his family. After he runs away towards the city centre, the final flashback occurs when he breaks into the Palace cinema.
Final flashback	This is a brief but extremely significant piece of flashback as it explains so much of Billy's past and the person he has become. His father has had only passing mention until now but assumes importance during Billy's remembrances of his time with him and the circumstances which led to his leaving the Casper household.
The world through Billy's eyes	The narrative is written in the third person, but the authorial viewpoint (see Literary Terms) is almost entirely that of Billy. The reader sees all events through Billy's eyes, and it is his perceptions of events and of other characters which are created. Billy's perceptions are extremely detailed and full. If we look at the description of the thrush pulling the worm from the ground on (p. 13), or the description of Mr Sugden preparing himself for the football match on (p. 92), we are not simply receiving Billy's impressions of what he sees. The author's viewpoint or impressions of people and environment are conveyed in these descriptive passages.

Realistic dialogue	Another technique the author employs is that of realistic dialogue, in particular the local dialect (see Literary Terms). This has the effect of making the conversations between characters realistic and natural, but also helps to reveal more about the interrelationships between characters.
The 'tall story'	Finally, there is Billy's 'tall story'. This becomes a natural part of the narrative as Billy writes it during his English lesson, but by positioning it just after Billy has revealed so much during his talk about Kes, the author uses it to show us a much broader picture of Billy's life. Simply by producing the story on the page without any authorial comment, its effectiveness as a commentary on Billy's life is increased. Every badly spelled incident in the story becomes for the reader a comment on what Billy lacks. By reproducing the bad spelling and punctuation, the author is able to make a further comment on Billy's lack of academic ability, in contrast with the expertise he has just shown, and also to make the story seem all the more realistic. It becomes a poignant commentary on the whole novel and is in many ways the focal point of the book. It mirrors the book's narrative structure, too: 'One day in the life'. This helps to reinforce the themes of the novel.

BILLY CASPER

Wild and untamed by home or school
Dishonest
Unloved
Patient and competent

Billy is overwhelmingly the main character in this novel, along with Kes who features in the title with him. In many ways they must be considered together.

In the conventional sense, Billy is one of life's losers. Academically he is a failure, being in the bottom stream of a secondary modern school, and about to leave school with no qualifications. He has problems with literacy and numeracy, and few social skills. He seems unable to function in the adult world; adults like Mr Porter, his employer, or Mrs Rose, the betting shop owner, regard him as a nuisance or a threat. He spends a lot of his time hating and being hated, swearing or making rude gestures at people, arguing, avoiding punishment.

He seems to be a natural victim. Macdowall and the other bullies at the school pick on him, taunting him because of his small size but also because he is less fortunate than they are. He seems underfed, undernourished in terms of love and kindness and a scapegoat for all of the naughtiest boys in the school. The teachers, especially Mr Gryce and Mr Sugden, seem almost to delight in singling out Billy for punishment. Even Mr Farthing is unsympathetic towards him when he is not paying attention in the lesson, and says that there is always somebody to spoil things, somebody you cannot suit. That somebody is Billy.

At home Billy is as much victim as he is at school. He is bullied by Jud, both physically and mentally. Mrs Casper does not appear to love him. He misses his father, but does not seem currently to see anything of him.

How much is Billy the one at fault?

Billy is clearly rude, careless of the feelings of others, and unwilling to make any effort to meet teachers, family or other adults half way. He is dishonest; he steals chocolate from Mr Porter, eggs and orange juice from the milkman, and a book from Priors bookshop. He has been in trouble with the police for breaking and entering, and his breaking into the Palace cinema shows how familiar this procedure is to him. He is deliberately destructive, he breaks the stolen eggs rather than eating them for breakfast, and trespasses on private land without a thought for the owners.

Billy has two sides to his character, depending where he is.

But this is one side of Billy. It seems to be shaped by his bleak home and school environment. The other is shaped by the natural world. Here Billy is at home. He is patient when he needs to be, hardworking, athletic and physically competent, and in total sympathy with the environment. He shows skill and expertise far beyond his years. But he is also wild in the sense that Kes is wild. He adapts to each environment as he finds it. He is in tune with Kes because, like himself, Kes is not tamed and does not care about anyone or anything. Both have the will to destroy, or to be destroyed, and at the end of the novel, tragically, both are destroyed. Kes is killed, but in a sense something is killed in Billy too, because only Kes enabled him to be his real self. It is significant that when hobbies are mentioned by the youth employment officer, Billy gets up and tries to run rather than tell the officer about his interests in wildlife. On one level, Billy has just realised what Jud may have done when he failed to find him, but on another level Kes does not even figure in his mind as a 'hobby', being almost part of him. She is the only thing he can trust. He trusts no person in his world, and at the end we are left with the feeling that he never will. His refusal to go down the mines suggests that at some level Billy is aware of the mismatch between himself and his

environment, but his inability to express himself clearly prevents him from getting the sort of work which might have kept him in touch with the natural world.
- Wild, untamed by home or school
- Rude and disruptive
- Dishonest, with a criminal record
- A victim, unloved and undernourished
- Skilled, patient and hardworking in training Kes
- Appreciates the natural world and is totally at home with nature

JUD

Foul-mouthed
bully
Violent and
callous

Jud is Billy's half brother, or so the novel hints when Macdowall taunts Billy in the playground with the fact that they are not like brothers. He is a rather one-sided character, in places almost a caricature (see Literary Terms).

Jud is a bully. He begins his day by thumping Billy who is smaller and younger, and pulling the blankets off him so that his sleep is disturbed. He treats Billy as his slave, expecting his under-age brother to put bets on for him, and only communicates with him by hitting and abusing him verbally.

He is crude and foul mouthed: 'Hands off cocks, on socks' are his opening words to Billy in the morning, and 'What's the matter wi'thee, shit th'bed?' when for once Billy is up early. His natural response to most situations seems to be swearing or violence.

He treats his mother almost as badly as he treats Billy, making disrespectful remarks about her sex life, taunting her about her behaviour when drunk, and refusing to do anything he is asked to around the house. He appears to treat her as a slave also. His attitudes to women seem generally disrespectful. He anticipates his night out (p. 37) as one where he will get drunk and see how far he can go sexually with the nearest available woman.

The question can be asked: is Jud realistic? Or is he a
caricature, too extreme to be convincing? Perhaps he
feels as deprived as Billy does by his mother's attitude,
and perhaps he, too, has always missed his own father,
and that has helped to make him into the
unsympathetic person he is. He is understandably
furious when Billy keeps the money and the bet wins.
What he says about having a week off work, had he
been able to collect the money, is the nearest we get to
an insight into Jud's mind: maybe he did not want to be
a miner any more than Billy does. However, the author
does not explore Jud's character in enough detail for the
reader to find out.

- A bully, often physically violent
- Disrespectful to adults, especially women
- Foul mouthed and verbally aggressive
- Unsympathetic and quick to anger

MRS CASPER

*Uncaring and
self-centred*

Billy's mother is another character in whom there seems
to be some element of caricature (see Literary Terms).
Is she really so bad as she is depicted?

Mrs Casper is a weak parent in many ways. She has
little or no control over either Jud or Billy. Jud appears
to frighten her, and she can do nothing when he kills
Billy's hawk. She does not behave in an appropriate
manner for a parent, asking Billy for a cigarette rather
than trying to persuade him not to smoke, and using
him as an errand boy when she knows that she has no
money for shopping and has not paid her debts. She
speaks to him in an aggressive and inappropriate
manner, often using foul language and making no
attempt to correct Billy's speech or manner. Indeed, his
manners are a reflection of hers. She makes no attempt
to get his meals, telling him to get his own, nor to
provide the essentials of civilised life such as a warm

house, or clean clothes. She appears embarrassed by any display of emotion from Billy. When he describes with enthusiasm how he is going to get and train a kestrel she does not even appear to be listening, and when Kes is killed she cannot comfort Billy and pushes him away. She seems uninterested in Billy and his concerns, though she is a bit more sympathetic towards Jud, perhaps because his interests coincide more closely with her own. She appears totally self-centred.

Mrs Casper is promiscuous and likes a good time. She goes out most nights and gets drunk, and seems to have a procession of men friends. This situation has clearly existed both before and since Billy's father left her. She makes no attempt to hide her sex life from her sons nor from anyone else, and Billy's 'uncles' are the talk of his classmates at school as well as of the estate in general.

- A careless parent: does not offer physical or emotional care
- Promiscuous and fond of drink
- A bad example to her sons
- Self-centred

MR FARTHING

Creance

Mr Farthing is the only character who shows any sympathy for Billy. This is because he is a more sympathetic person, with a more humane approach to others, than any adult whom Billy encounters.

From the start of the lesson where he is described, Mr Farthing is shown empathising with the boys who have been caned, suggesting that he does not really approve of physical punishment. He is concerned at the lack of basic literacy in the boys and is doing his best to improve their skills by engaging them in ways they will find interesting. He uses talk and the boys' own experiences as his way into the lesson, and when

Not afraid to
learn as well as
teach
Firm and fair-
minded

Anderson is telling his story about the tadpoles he is
listening for the interesting content and responding to
Anderson rather than looking for errors in vocabulary.
He does become impatient with Billy when he is not
listening, but is willing to listen to Billy's point of view
after the fight at break when they talk.

Mr Farthing is strict and will stand no nonsense: when
he calls for quiet and moves towards the boys they are
silent. He breaks up the fight in a way which suggests
that he can easily exert his authority over the toughest
of the boys. He is also fair. He will not tolerate
Macdowall bullying Billy because he is smaller and
more vulnerable. He is forceful in making this point,
and shows Macdowall what it is like to be bullied by
picking on him physically. Mr Farthing does not always
use the most conventional method to teach the boys
(would being physically violent towards Macdowall be
tolerated in a teacher today?)

Mr Farthing
appears to be
the only teacher
at Billy's school
who is not
time-serving.

He does not patronise or talk down to the boys
although he often has to explain things to them in
simple terms. Though Billy is among the least able
academically, Mr Farthing learns something from him
when he talks about Kes. He is happy to admit that he
can learn from his pupils as well as the other way
round, and when he comes to watch Kes flying at lunch-
time he does not talk down to Billy. Their conversation
(on pp. 114–19) is adult to adult with Mr Farthing
using the same ideas and vocabulary as he would to
anyone of equal intelligence and social standing.

- Firm but fair: does not tolerate bullying or
  indiscipline
- Enjoys teaching and makes lessons as interesting and
  relevant as he can
- Not afraid to learn as well as teach; respects Billy's
  expertise
- Interested in the boys as people

MR SUGDEN

Self-important
Obsessive
Sadistic

Mr Sugden, the games master, is both an amusing character and another bully, an adult one this time. The lengthy episode in the novel in which he appears consists of the games lesson and football match followed by the incident in the showers.

Mr Sugden enjoys victimising the boys who are not interested or good at games, like Billy. He deliberately uses vocabulary that Billy does not understand when he tells him off for being late, and assumes that Billy is deliberately trying to get out of the lesson even though he has a legitimate excuse for being late. He taunts Billy and imitates him for the entertainment of the other boys when he says that he has no kit. When Billy answers back, Sugden steps up the intimidation, and becomes physically violent. He uses the oversized pair of shorts to make further fun of Billy.

Mr Sugden's teaching is more about showing off his own footballing prowess than improving the skills of the boys. His method of choosing teams is guaranteed to humiliate the least able footballers like Billy. (Does he do this deliberately, or is he just unaware?) He is very proud of the way he is dressed in perfect Manchester United colours, and spends much time preening himself before the match begins. He will allow only one opinion – his own – and threatens Tibbut with being sent off when he tries to argue with him.

Mr Sugden is now past his prime as a footballer, but he is determined to win the match by fair means or foul. He cheats deliberately, in a way he would never tolerate in the pupils, but they are expected to accept it because he is the teacher. When Billy, hopeless in goal, distracts himself and others by athletic antics on the cross-bar, Mr Sugden is furious, and when Billy fails to save a goal he pushes him into the mud. He does not in any way encourage Billy who is obviously quite talented athletically, nor does he show any appreciation of Billy's skill with animals when he manages to lead the dog away from the field. When Billy tells him that he forgot to swap sittings he shows no sympathy, telling him to forget about his dinner too.

At the end of the match and in the showers, Mr Sugden shows the darker side of his nature. Until now he has been amusing, but towards the end of the match his behaviour is obsessive. In the showers he takes out his anger on Billy in a deliberately sadistic way by hitting him, forcing him into the showers, then posting guards and turning the water to cold until Billy is freezing. He seems incapable of appreciating what one of the boys says, that it was only a game. He deliberately seeks revenge on Billy, who seems to represent for him all the frustration he feels as a teacher in a secondary modern school, and possibly a failed professional footballer. There is certainly some element of caricature in the author's portrayal of Sugden, as there is in Jud and Mrs Casper, but he seems to represent much that the author finds at fault in teachers.

- Amusing, but a bully
- Obsessive about the football match
- Sadistic in his treatment of Billy and other boys who are bad at games
- Self-opinioned and self-important
- A caricature, rather than a fully rounded character

MR GRYCE

Out of touch with his pupils

Neurotic and obsessive

As the headmaster of Billy's school Mr Gryce is an important character, though his appearance in the novel is fairly brief. He is used by the author, as are all the teachers, to convey his views on the education Billy receives.

Mr Gryce appears in assembly, where he refuses to tolerate the standard of singing, and shouts at the boys for coughing. On one hand he seems to be insisting on high standards in his school, but he is obsessed with minor details and gets angry about involuntary actions like coughing which are difficult to control. When someone coughs again after his furious start to assembly, Mr Gryce has no way of catching the culprit, so he puts his staff under pressure by yelling at Mr Crossley to find the boy. This guarantees that Mr Crossley will find somebody, preferably a known troublemaker like Macdowall, and so Gryce gets what he wants, but it is clearly unjust.

The almost ritual caning which takes place after each morning assembly is a feature of Mr Gryce's school. He has three smokers, Macdowall who allegedly coughed, and Billy who fell asleep on his feet, as a typical line up on the morning of the day described. He is cynical and weary in his attitude to the boys, declaiming in a diatribe against young people that not a day goes by without his having to cane a line of them, but unable to understand that it could be a fault in their education which is the cause. He is clearly out of touch with the boys' lives and despises much of the culture of young people without making any attempt to understand it. He looks back with nostalgia to the 'good old days' when, even though times were hard, boys respected their elders.

In some ways we can feel some sympathy for Mr Gryce who cannot understand the modern world. He hates the lack of discipline and the fact that boys and their parents are readier to complain and shout about their rights. However, his complete lack of understanding of the boys and his inability to listen to anyone else's views work against him. He does not listen to anyone once he is in full flight: the poor little boy who brought the message from Mr Crossley gets the cane along with the line of boys sent there for it! Although the author paints an amusing picture here, Billy's conversation with Mr Farthing after the fight makes it clear that his sympathies lie with the small boy.

Think whether Mr Gryce is a rounded character or more of a caricature.

Mr Gryce makes a later, brief appearance when Billy emerges after hiding from Jud and is on his way to his youth employment interview. Here he is as unsympathetic towards Billy as anyone in the novel, and completely fails to give him much-needed encouragement on his way to the interview which may determine his future. The last mention of Gryce shows him cuffing a small boy on the side of the head for walking on the wrong side of the corridor. He is obsessed with trivial details but does not seem to see the things which are important in the lives of his pupils.

• Strict, but out-of-touch with pupils
• Concerned with details but does not see important issues
• Does not listen to the boys
• Self-important
• Looks back often to the 'good old days'

Most of the remaining characters in the novel make only very brief appearances as Billy comes into contact with them at some point in his day.

Mr Porter

Billy's employer, the newsagent. He is prejudiced against boys from the council estate where Billy lives, and distrusts Billy. Critical of everything he does, he gets little respect from Billy in return, and is always threatening to sack him and employ a more middle-class boy.

Tibbut

Once Billy's friend, or as near to it as Billy gets. He now distrusts Billy because since getting Kes Billy no longer hangs about with Macdowall's gang getting into trouble, and blames Billy's training of Kes as the cause.

Macdowall

Macdowall is the school bully, large, aggressive and used to intimidating the others. He is the leader of the gang which Billy used to mix with before getting Kes, and clearly resents Billy's defection. He selects his victims from the vulnerable, and is known by the teachers as a troublemaker.

The farmer

At first the owner of Monastery Farm is angry with Billy for trespassing on his land, but when he realises that Billy's interest in the kestrels is genuine, he is more sympathetic and lets him look more closely at the nest. He advises him to read about falconry out of concern for the birds, as he says it is cruel if they are badly kept.

Mrs rose

The betting shop owner's wife is totally unsympathetic towards Billy, seeing the incident with the betting money as totally his fault. She is worried by characters like Jud and has clearly had a hard time with him.

Youth employment officer

The officer seems to be going through the motions with Billy and many of the school leavers, recommending a prepared series of options and going through his speech without adapting it to the needs of individual boys. It is somewhat ridiculous for him to recommend degrees to a boy who has difficulty with basic reading and writing! He is irritated with Billy because he does not react as he would expect.

THE LIBRARIAN

She classifies Billy according to his appearance and where he lives, and is not going to make it easy for him to join the library. She fails to understand his home difficulties or his sudden need for a book, and refuses to bend the rules even so far as to let him look at one.

BILLY S FATHER

Billy's father is a shadowy figure who has left home before the novel opens. The only real picture of him comes from the flashback (see Literary Terms) in the cinema. We see a man who was fond of Billy and took him out, but who refused to tolerate his wife's infidelity. Billy has missed him ever since, but does not talk about him. Only in his 'tall story' does he mention how much he misses him.

MRS CROSSLEY AND THE MATHEMATICS TEACHER

These teachers have some contact with Billy during the day: Crossley at registration and the mathematics teacher after lunch. Both treat him with distant lack of sympathy and Crossley with anger because he messes up his register. The staff are under pressure from the head teacher to get the surface details right so cannot have any time left for the boys. Billy complains to Mr Farthing that these two and other teachers are always looking at their watches to see how long it is to the end of the lesson, and calling them insulting names like 'numbskulls' and 'cretins'. They appear not to care about their pupils at all and treat the job as a means of earning money only.

THE THREE SMOKERS AND OTHER PUPILS

The three boys caught smoking are typical pupils at Billy's school: disillusioned, making little effort with work, looking forward only to leaving. They resent the attitudes of Mr Gryce and many of the staff, and seem to feel that they are too old for school.

THE MESSENGER

This boy is young enough still to feel that school is worthwhile, to work hard, and show willing, but he learns a bitter lesson. Forced by his fear of the smokers into accepting their cigarettes and lighters, he is caned when Gryce refuses to listen to him, and in any case he dare not tell the truth.

THE NEIGHBOURS

These people almost seem to act as a chorus (see Literary Terms) commenting on events in Billy's home. They appear at their doorsteps when there is trouble to gape at, but not to help. One woman, asked by a distraught Billy whether she has seen Jud, fails to notice how upset he is and remarks to herself, 'Eeh, what a family that is!'

LANGUAGE & STYLE

The style and language in which this novel is written combines very formal, detailed descriptive passages with a lively narrative of the incidents involving people, including realistic dialogue using Yorkshire dialect (see Literary Terms).

Description   The descriptive passages depict Billy's environment in various ways:

- Billy's responses to the natural world and his powers of observation are shown in the descriptions of the woods, nesting, the farm, moors and fields as he delivers papers.

- During the flashback (see Literary Terms) when Billy goes nesting one morning and discovers the kestrel's nest, there is a vivid description of the early morning atmosphere in the fields.
- The descriptions are not sentimental (see Literary Terms) or idealised: Kes is described graphically as she eats the sparrow Billy has shot to feed her, even down to the 'slithering putty coloured pile' of intestines.

There is also much description in the novel of the effects of people on the environment:

- The 'only clean feature' of the school is the silver birch outside the head teacher's study; the rest has been built on and ruined.
- There is graphic description of the estate, where seeded verges have been run over and dog holes made in fences.
- The description of the fight in the playground uses metaphor (see Literary Terms) to focus on the boys almost as if they were wildlife being observed by the author: a technique he often uses. Another example of this is the description of the boys playing football, and of the rest of the school leaving the building when the bell goes for the lesson end.

Then there is description of people which helps to convey the author's attitude to them, for example the description of Sugden's boots: 'Polished as black and shiny as the bombs used by assassins in comic strips'. This is amusing, and refers to familiar aspects of Billy's life and that of boys like him, but also hints at Sugden's sadistic nature.

Dialogue   Incidents are conveyed to the reader in a lively way through this description but also through the dialogue. Much of this is made realistic by the use of local Yorkshire dialect (see Literary Terms), for example,

Anderson's story about the tadpoles. At times the dialect adds to the tone and atmosphere (see Literary Terms) of conversation, for example, the violence of much of the interaction between the Casper family. Jud's profanities are a clue to his character, as is the way Mrs Casper speaks.

Some of the dialogue highlights the contrast between the worlds of different characters, for example, in the conversations between Billy and Mr Farthing, when the teacher's use of standard English is contrasted with Billy's use of dialect. In their first conversation, after the playground fight, Billy is at a disadvantage, but in their second talk after Billy has just demonstrated flying Kes to Mr Farthing, the teacher is all admiration for Billy's skill, and the gap between their language seems less, with Billy responding with understanding to Mr Farthing's ideas about the hawk demanding instinctive respect from people. They are on the same wavelength and their use of language becomes more similar.

Imagery   Billy Hines used Billy's bubble-blowing (p. 86) as a symbol (see Literary Terms). Note the similarities between the description of the beautiful bubbles-like 'a jewel', riding the air, only to vanish – and Kes.

PART FOUR

STUDY SKILLS

HOW TO USE QUOTATIONS

One of the secrets of success in writing essays is the way you use quotations. There are five basic principles:

- Put inverted commas at the beginning and end of the quotation
- Write the quotation exactly as it appears in the original
- Do not use a quotation that repeats what you have just written
- Use the quotation so that it fits into your sentence
- Keep the quotation as short as possible

Quotations should be used to develop the line of thought in your essays.

Your comment should not duplicate what is in the question. For example:

Billy explains to Mr Farthing that he always seems to get into trouble for very little, although he is no worse than many other boys, 'I don't know, Sir, I just seem to get into bother for nowt. You know, for daft things, like this morning in t'hall'.

Far more effective is to write:

Billy explains that 'I just seem to get into bother for nowt. You know, for daft things, like this morning in' t'hall'.

However, the most sophisticated way of using the writer's words is to embed them into your sentence:

The fact that Sugden bounces the ball on Billy's head 'as though he was murdering him with a boulder' demonstrates what a sadistic bully he can be.

When you use quotations in this way, you are demonstrating the ability to use text as evidence to support your ideas - not simply including words from the original to prove you have read it.

Everyone writes differently. Work through the suggestions given here and adapt the advice to suit your own style and interests. This will improve your essay-writing skills and allow your personal voice to emerge.

The following points indicate in ascending order the skills of essay writing:

- Picking out one or two facts about the story and adding the odd detail
- Writing about the text by retelling the story
- Retelling the story and adding a quotation here and there
- Organising an answer which explains what is happening in the text and giving quotations to support what you write

....

- Writing in such a way as to show that you have thought about the intentions of the writer of the text and that you understand the techniques used
- Writing at some length, giving your viewpoint on the text and commenting by picking out details to support your views
- Looking at the text as a work of art, demonstrating clear critical judgement and explaining to the reader of your essay how the enjoyment of the text is assisted by literary devices, linguistic effects and psychological insights; showing how the text relates to the time when it was written

The dotted line above represents the division between lower- and higher-level grades. Higher-level performance begins when you start to consider your response as a reader of the text. The highest level is reached when you offer an enthusiastic personal response and show how this piece of literature is a product of its time.

Coursework essay

Set aside an hour or so at the start of your work to plan what you have to do.

- List all the points you feel are needed to cover the task. Collect page references of information and quotations that will support what you have to say. A helpful tool is the highlighter pen: this saves painstaking copying and enables you to target precisely what you want to use.

- Focus on what you consider to be the main points of the essay. Try to sum up your argument in a single sentence, which could be the closing sentence of your essay. Depending on the essay title, it could be a statement about a character: Mr Gryce and Mr Sugden are both characters who care very little about the boys they teach, as they fail to listen to them or to see things from their point of view; an opinion about a setting: The woods and area around Monastery farm are vitally significant in Billy Casper's, life, because it is there that he encounters the natural world which is so important to him and it is from there that he gets Kes who is the only thing he can trust; or a judgement on a theme: An important theme in *A Kestrel for a Knave* is how the environment shapes a person's character, because the Casper family seem to be adversely affected by their home environment and the boys at Billy's school seem to be affected by the education they receive.

- Make a short essay plan. Use the first paragraph to introduce the argument you wish to make. In the following paragraphs develop this argument with details, examples and other possible points of view. Sum up your argument in the last paragraph. Check you have answered the question.

- Write the essay, remembering all the time the central point you are making.

- On completion, go back over what you have written

to eliminate careless errors and improve expression. Read it aloud to yourself, or, if you are feeling more confident, to a relative or friend.

If you can, try to type your essay using a word processor. This will allow you to correct and improve your writing without spoiling its appearance.

Examination essay

The essay written in an examination often carries more marks than the coursework essay even though it is written under considerable time pressure.

In the revision period build up notes on various aspects of the text you are using. Fortunately, in acquiring this set of York Notes on *A Kestrel for a Knave,* you have made a prudent beginning! York Notes are set out to give you vital information and help you to construct your personal overview of the text.

Make notes with appropriate quotations about the key issues of the set text. Go into the examination knowing your text and having a clear set of opinions about it.

In most English Literature examinations you can take in copies of your set books. This is an enormous advantage although it may lull you into a false sense of security. Beware! There is simply not enough time in an examination to read the book from scratch.

In the examination

- Read the question paper carefully and remind yourself what you have to do.
- Look at the questions on your set texts to select the one that most interests you and mentally work out the points you wish to stress.
- Remind yourself of the time available and how you are going to use it.
- Briefly map out a short plan in note form that will keep your writing on track and illustrate the key argument you want to make.

- Then set about writing it.
- When you have finished, check through to eliminate errors.

To summarise, these are the keys to success
- **Know the text**
- **Have a clear understanding of and opinions on the storyline, characters, setting, themes and writer's concerns**
- **Select the right material**
- **Plan and write a clear response, continually bearing the question in mind**

SAMPLE ESSAY PLAN

A typical essay question on *A Kestrel for a Knave* is followed by a sample essay plan in note form. This does not present the only answer to the question, merely one answer. Do not be afraid to include your own ideas and leave out some of the ones in this sample! Remember that quotations are essential to prove and illustrate the points you make.

Remind yourself of Billy's 'tall story' (on p. 73 of the text). Why is this important to the themes of the novel and what does it tell us about Billy Casper's life?

Introduction
Tall story very important; at centre of novel because it helps the reader focus on Billy's environment and how it affects him.

Home and school dealt with in story; Billy's ideal day.

Part 1
Tall story describes a typical day Billy would like to have, unlike other boys who may have written fantasy etc.

For many boys of his age what happens would be normal, not a tall story.

Spelling and punctuation left as Billy would use it: deliberate authorial technique to make point about deprivation more strongly.

Part 2   Home environment: in story Billy lives up on Moor
                  Edge; where he delivers papers & looks enviously in at
                  others' houses.

                  They have carpets and central heating: contrast with
                  Billy's real house; on council estate in town, not in
                  pleasant enviroment; no curtains, poor furnishing.

                  Mother brings Billy breakfast in bed: in reality Billy
                  gets up, lights fire, no breakfast and Jud has taken milk.

                  Sun shines outside in story: Billy gets up in the dark to
                  do paper round.

                  In story Jud has joined the army: wishful thinking as he
                  bullies Billy (give some examples).

                  Father returns: again wishful thinking: father left after
                  mother's infidelity; Billy misses him and vividly
                  remembers his packing his case after the row and taking
                  it away.

Part 3   Billy's mother works and neglects him: in story she
                  announces that she is not going to work any more. Give
                  examples of neglect: physical (no meals etc.) and
                  emotional (lack of understanding, of enthusiasm for
                  Kes; inability to cope with situation when Jud kills
                  Kes). In story the family goes to the cinema: no family
                  outings in reality, and no treats such as ice cream or fish
                  and chips for supper.

Part 4   School environment: in story teachers take an interest
                  in Billy and show affection 'patted me on the head'.
                  They are good to him. In reality teachers harsh and
                  uninterested or actively hostile: give examples, e.g. Mr
                  Gryce and the caning Billy has just had, and the way
                  Mr Sugden treats him in lesson and in showers
                  afterwards.

Conclusion   Complete contrast between tall story and reality shows
                  how deprived Billy's environment is both at home and

at school, and how he would like to live but knows to be impossible. Authorial technique of including story without any authorial comment makes the point all the more poignantly, and draws the contrast more sharply. Tall story reflects narrative structure of day in the life of Billy, and thus underlines the book's theme of how Billy is being destroyed by his environment.

FURTHER QUESTIONS

Make a plan as shown above and attempt these questions:

1 Since writing the novel, Barry Hines has said that he was unfair in his portrayal of Jud and Mrs Casper. Do you agree with him and, if so, in what particular respects might Hines feel the portrayal to be unfair?

2 What does Billy gain from his experience of school, and what does he gain from his self-education outside school? How is he different inside and outside school?

3 Choose TWO incidents in the novel which you found amusing. Write about them, pointing out why you found them humorous.

4 Is it true that the society in which he lives has not done a great deal for Billy? And is it not also true that Billy has not done much to help himself?

PART FIVE

CULTURAL CONNECTIONS

BROADER PERSPECTIVES

The film Kes   In 1970, not long after *A Kestrel for a Knave* was published, it was made into a very successful film by director Ken Loach. The novel lends itself to film because of its structure and the use of flashback technique, and you will probably enjoy watching it. There are one or two extra scenes in the film which are not in the book, but which give you further insight into the Casper family life, especially that of Jud and Mrs Casper. Barry Hines was involved in the screenplay for the film, and perhaps these scenes were an attempt to be fairer to these two characters and make them more rounded and believable people.

Other books   You may enjoy these other books and find them relevant to the themes of *A Kestrel for a Knave*:

Our Day Out, a play by Willy Russell (Methuen, 1984) is also about the effect of environment on a class of deprived and academically poor children. They are taken by their teacher, Mrs Kay, on a day trip to Wales, to give them a good day out, but a stricter teacher, Mr Briggs, comes along to keep order.

Buddy by Nigel Hinton (Heinemann, 1982) is another novel that deals with adolescence and a boy growing up in difficult circumstances. Buddy's mother leaves home and he and his father have to manage without her.

Jane Eyre by Charlotte Brontë was written in the 1840s. Jane has to deal with an unhappy home environment and then is sent away to school where life is no easier for her at first. She is a spirited independent girl who eventually finds happiness after many difficulties. A recent film of the novel should make enjoyable viewing in conjunction with your reading.

'Timothy Winters' by Charles Causley is a poem which can be found in *New Dragon Book of Verse* (p. 113). Timothy, like Billy, has a difficult home environment which is depicted in this poem. But he is a very different character.

anecdote narrative of small incident or event, told for entertainment or to reveal character. Used by Mr Farthing in his 'Fact and Fiction' lesson when Anderson and Billy tell their own anecdotes

atmosphere the mood in a particular piece of writing, for example, the calm, serene mood established by Barry Hines in his descriptions of the fields early in the morning

caricature a character who seems almost ludicrous because his or her behaviour is exaggeratedly good or bad: Jud or Mrs Casper might fit into that category

chorus in Ancient Greek drama, the chorus was a group of ordinary bystanders who commented on the action of the play

dialect the way of speaking in a particular district

diatribe an angry or uncontrolled verbal attack on something, like Mr Gryce's attack on young people

episodic a narrative which is written in the form of a series of separable incidents

flashback a term borrowed from film, to describe a sudden jump backwards in time to an earlier period of the character's life

metaphor goes further than a comparison between two different things by fusing them together; one thing is described as being another

narrative, third person telling of a story decribing the characters as 'he', 'she' or 'they'

point of view/authorial viewpoint the way an author approaches his/her characters, and the reader. Whose view of events are we shown? Is it always Billy's, or does the author observe and comment on events separately?

realism telling things as they are, often with haphazard detail, evoking real experiences. Rather vague as a term, but much of the writing in *A Kestrel for a Knave* could be said to be realistic

round character someone who develops and changes during the course of the novel. Billy could be said to develop through his relationship with Kes, but Mrs Casper does not

sarcasm a bitter or wounding remark, intended to hurt

sentimental often used to indicate an excess of feeling, inappropriately used. Hines's descriptions are not sentimental because they are true to nature and describe things as they are

symbol a material object used to represent something invisible like an idea or quality

TEST ANSWERS